*Quick*GUIDES

everything you need to know...fast

FUNDRAISING DATABASES
Adapting for Different Needs

by Peter Flory

reviewed by Caroline Hukins

WIREMILL
PUBLISHING LTD

Across the world the organizations and institutions that fundraise to finance their work are referred to in many different ways. They are charities, non-profits or not-for-profit organizations, non-governmental organizations (NGOs), voluntary organizations, academic institutions, agencies, etc. For ease of reading, we have used the term Nonprofit Organization, Organization or NPO as an umbrella term throughout the *Quick* Guide series. We have also used the spellings and punctuation used by the author.

Published by
Wiremill Publishing Ltd.
Edenbridge, Kent TN8 5PS, UK
info@wiremillpublishing.com
www.wiremillpublishing.com
www.quickguidesonline.com

British Library Cataloguing in Publication Data
A catalogue record for this book is available from the British Library.

ISBN Number 1-905053-11-8

Printed by Rhythm Consolidated Berhad, Malaysia
Cover Design by Jennie de Lima and Edward Way
Design by Colin Woodman Design

Disclaimer of Liability
The author, reviewer and publisher shall have neither liability nor responsibility to any person or entity with respect to any loss or damage caused or alleged to be caused directly or indirectly by the information contained in this book. While the book is as accurate as possible, there may be errors, omissions or inaccuracies.

Contents

Introduction

The *Quick*Guide *Fundraising Databases: An Introduction to the Setup and Use* gives a general introduction to this subject. This *Quick*Guide is designed to give a more detailed and technical discussion of the diverse needs of a database. In particular, it discusses the differences that are required for different user groups within an organisation.

This book illustrates how the database can accommodate the needs of corporate fundraising, trusts, high value donors and other special relationships, events, individual supporters, campaigns, bequests, and other disciplines. Each section details the technical points that need to be considered when setting up and managing the database. This *Quick*Guide is intended as a starting point to help you consider all the functions that you will need in each area. The specific requirements, however, will be unique to each nonprofit organisation (NPO). It is impossible to give universal or definitive lists of data fields, reports or functions.

HOW CAN THE DATABASE HELP?

Because approaches to companies and grantmakers happen over a long period of time and the relationships continue over a long period of time, the database should be able to keep a record of all actions taken and communications effected during the course of a relationship with a grantmaker or company. It can record intended future actions and prompt the user at the correct time. Clearly it must record all income, both pledged and actual. It should record links in all directions among individuals, grantmakers and companies. It would be helpful to be able to search such criteria as interest in a certain project, potential to give, company size, geographical area of support, and many more.

TECHNICAL CONSIDERATIONS

A number of special data items are required for this type of fundraising, which are not needed for other types of supporter. For example:

- Details of the company or grantmaker.
- Details of your contact at the company or grantmaker.
- What type of support they will give.

- What projects they will support.
- Geographic areas they will support.
- The amount they are likely to give.
- When you can contact them/apply for funds.
- What you have to supply to them (e.g., annual report, audited accounts, etc.).
- Reporting requirements.
- Ongoing contacts.

As opposed to a one-off direct mail campaign, an approach to a company or grantmaker usually consists of a series of communications over a period of time. This demands a recording of a history or log of communications. It is essential to know what was said to whom, by whom and when. Data items recorded for these communications include:

- Date.
- Action (letter, email, telephone call, meeting, visit, lunch, dinner, etc.).
- Direction of action (from supporter to you or from you to supporter).

Continues on next page

- Subject.

- Status.

- Result.

- General notes.

A diary facility is useful to record future actions. Against each action, record who is responsible for the action. You also need the ability to postpone actions and transfer the responsibility for actions to other members of staff.

A useful feature is having an "auto-remind" function so that when you turn your computer on, it shows the actions for completion that day relating to each company or grantmaker. It will also show any actions that are overdue. To do this requires a status indicator to be associated with each action.

These individual campaigns may result in immediate support; more frequently, they will result in "pledges", either a promise of money or other support in the future or payment of a promised amount over a period of time.

A grant or donation can be a single amount that is promised on or by a specified date, or it can be a multi-payment support with several amounts and specified dates. In either case, the database must record the details. Thus, the situation can be monitored and follow-up letters sent or telephone calls made if the money does not come in on time. Recording due dates with amounts also helps to produce income-flow forecasts.

Other requirements are:

- Maintenance of a running "balance" for multi-payment support (what has come in compared with what is still to come).

- The ability to alter amounts and dates and even write off balances that are not going to be fulfilled.

In addition to recording actions, grants and income, the database must record details of donations that are not "real" money but have a notional monetary value. These are such things as gifts in kind, loan of staff, sponsorship of expenditure (e.g., paying for the printing of a booklet), help at events, personal appearances, etc.

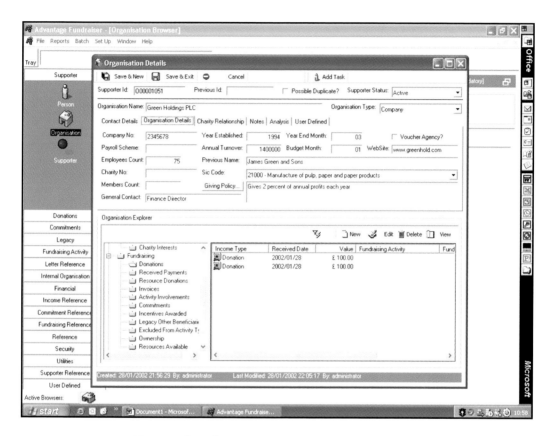

Example of company information from database Advantage Fundraiser

High Value Donors and Other Special Relationships

How Can the Database Help?

Trustees, high value donors, bequest or legacy pledgers, celebrities, members of parliament, press and other media contacts, volunteers and beneficiaries all require special care. They may need to be excluded from standard database functions, and their confidential information will need to be stored very securely.

Technical Considerations

A number of in-built database features can help to manage these relationships efficiently and effectively. In order to make best use of the database, the following functions need to be considered:

- Recording special data items that are not required for normal supporters, such as their wealth, their capacity to give, when you can contact them, whether contact is direct or through a third party, what type of projects they will support, what type of support they will give and where they will give it, what they expect in return, how often you can approach them.

- Being able to record all the relationships these people have with other people and organisations (e.g., peer groups or involvement with grantmaking bodies, directors and companies).

- Being able to contact these people via third parties (particularly for celebrities) rather than directly which requires different addresses, links between people and the ability to decide which address (or telephone number, or email address) is used in which circumstance.

- Allocating the responsibility for contacting each of these people to one particular person in your organisation and ensuring that all communication goes via this person.

- Excluding these people from standard selections and mailings (for example, you do not want to send someone several small appeals per year if they normally give you one large donation a year).

■ Excluding these people from standard fulfilment. When they do send you money you want to send them a personal letter and not a standard mail-merged thank you letter.

■ Having security procedures to restrict different users' access to the system so that only people who are entitled to access and use the information on these special people are the ones who do so.

Reviewer's Comment

All supporters of your organisation are important, but high value donors require a level of personal contact and relationship building that can be greatly aided by a properly planned and implemented database.

All the special relationships referred to in this chapter are more easily and efficiently catered for by an appropriate database that is properly and fully used.

Continues on next page

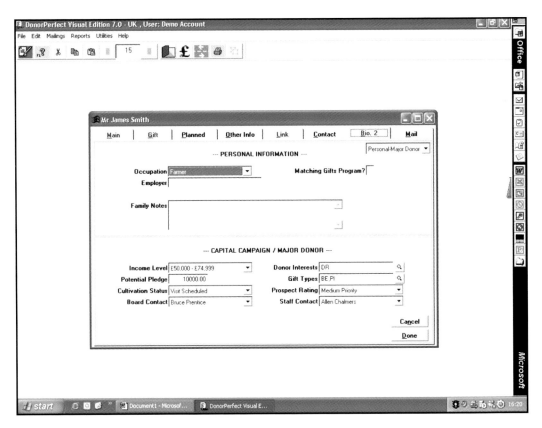

Example of major donor information from database DonorPerfect

INDIVIDUAL SUPPORTERS AND COMMITTED GIVERS

How Can the Database Help?

When supporters show commitment to your cause and give to your organisation regularly, the database can provide great assistance in managing the processes involved. The most common methods are membership, subscriptions, regular payments, payroll giving and corporate gift matching.

Technical Considerations

Membership

Membership is usually managed on an annual basis, and database functions can include: maintaining different types of members with different rates/fee structures, sending reminders when fees are due, collecting fees, printing invoices/thank you letters, sending follow-up letters, printing membership cards, calculating member statistics, maintaining membership status, printing lists of different types of members.

Subscriptions

Subscriptions processing is the management of the process of a supporter paying for a regular service or publication. There is a great deal of overlap with membership processing (e.g., payment reminders, collecting fees, printing invoices/thank you letters, sending follow-up letters), and the function is often combined with membership processing because "members" almost always get a regular publication for their money.

Standing orders

Standing orders are regular amounts (usually monthly) given by the supporter, which are initiated by the supporter's bank on his or her behalf. If you have a lot of them the database should have the ability to import the income items from a file supplied by your bank. This saves you having to key the same items into the database every single month. The database will then be able to print two fundamental reports: (1) the amount expected but not received and (2) the amount received but not expected.

Direct debits

Direct debits are regular payments that the supporter has agreed to make to

Continues on next page

your organisation, except that your organisation initiates the process and claims the payments from the bank. The database needs to be able to create a file of these payments to send to the bank, enter the payments against the supporters; and reconcile and report on any differences when notice of payments made is received from the bank.

Reviewer's Comment

Standing orders and direct debits are particular kinds of regular payments found in some countries under a variety of names. Other regular payments that may be found in your own country will benefit from similar database considerations.

Payroll giving

Payroll giving is when regular payments are made to your organisation directly from the supporter's salary, usually paid to you directly by the supporter's employer. The database needs to record the supporters; the employers; the agencies, if any, that process the payments; the amounts expected and the amounts received.

Corporate gift matching

When a company pledges to match the amounts that its employees give to you, the database needs to record the running total of the amounts received from the employees and reconcile and report on the amounts received from the employer. It also needs to prompt you for anything required by you.

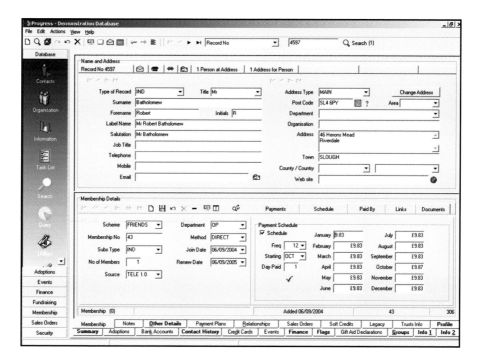

**Membership payment schedule from
database Progress**

How Can the Database Help?

Organisations run events of many different types, and a good events management module in the database is essential to help manage and monitor them. Events can require a database to hold a lot of information that is not relevant to other fundraising disciplines. If the central database does not have such functions, then it is likely that parallel systems will be developed, resulting in duplication of function and information storage.

Technical Considerations

With the right data structure in place, the following functions can be performed by the database:

- Selections can be made to invite people to an event, and these invitations recorded.

- Acceptances can be recorded and bookings made.

- Invoices can be issued.

- Waiting lists can be maintained if the event is oversubscribed.

- Cancellations can be made and refunds issued.

- Meal choices or special requirements can be recorded and lists produced.

- Name badges can be printed.

- Many essential reports and lists can be produced (e.g., delegate lists, session lists, helper lists, payments due, cumulative profit, costs paid and costs outstanding).

- Attendees of one event can be mailed with details of another.

- Thank you letters, receipts, and tickets can be produced, in bulk or individually.

- Donations in lieu of attendance can be recorded and linked to the event.

- Time plans can be drafted, and reminders programmed in.

- Specific events or promotions can be reported on and analysed.

- Income, events and different promotions can be evaluated in detail.

EVENTS

The term "event" embraces a range of different activities, such as fundraising events, conferences, donor cultivation events and publicity launches. For the database, however, there are two basic types of events to consider: (1) the event organised by the NPO itself and (2) the event organised by a supporter from which the NPO receives the proceeds.

For the first type of event, the database must maintain a table of data about the event itself. Linked to this table will be tables of all the other relevant information. For example:

- Planning actions in a diary format.
- Venues.
- Sessions within the event.
- Costs.
- Prices for delegates to attend.
- Equipment required.
- Helpers/organizers.
- Speakers or celebrity guests.

- Attendees.
- Information sent to participants/ attendees.
- Medical details.
- Special requirements/diet.

For the fundraising event organised by a supporter, very little information is required about the event but the additional functions required are:

- Against the supporter, record the nature of the event, the date and the expected income.
- Record details of sponsors and the amount they pledged if the supporter is being sponsored to carry out an activity.
- Record details of promotional items sent to the supporter.
- Record income received.
- Send reminder letters if no money is received after a specified time period.

Continues on next page

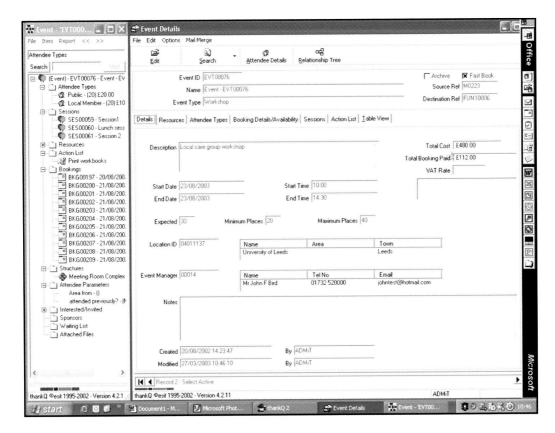

**Event management data from
database thankQ**

HOW CAN THE DATABASE HELP?

The database must have special procedures to deal with other types of income, such as gifts at death (bequests or legacies), in memoriam donations, sponsorships and gifts in kind (GIKs).

TECHNICAL CONSIDERATIONS

Bequests or legacies

The administration of gifts at death can be a complex business carried out over a long period of time. The database can help you keep track of where things are and what needs to be done next. Bequest or legacy administration starts with marketing. The database will need to record who has been sent information, who has made an enquiry, and who has actually said they have included the organisation in their Will or Codicil. Once an organisation has been informed that it is mentioned in a Will, then information such as the type of legacy, the projected amount, the other beneficiaries, the executors, and payments made will need to be recorded and monitored.

In memoriam donations

Gifts given in memory of a deceased person need additional data recorded with them in order that you know whom the gift was from and for whom it was given in memory – soft credits will help here.

Reviewer's Comment

Soft credits are database entries that reflect both the actual donor and the person on whose behalf the donation was made.

Gifts in kind

Gifts in kind, whether they are donated goods or donated time, have a notional value. All the details relating to the donation need to be recorded and summarised (but not included in income figures transferred to accounts).

Sponsorship

Similarly, sponsorship needs to be recorded, as in the case of a company paying directly for items that the NPO would otherwise have to purchase, such

Continues on next page

as the printing of a newsletter or costs of an event. This does not constitute funds received by the organisation, but it does have a "notional" value in reducing expenditure. Again, it needs to be recorded and summarised, but not included in income figures transferred to accounts.

Raffles

Some NPOs run raffles where tickets are sent to supporters to sell. The ticket numbers need to be recorded against the people to whom they were sent, along with details of the tickets returned and the people who purchased them.

Trading and sales

Many organisations make money from sales. Sales may be of holiday cards, items branded with the organisation's logo, merchandise related to the organisation's activities or anything else that raises funds for the organisation. A sales order-processing module and a stock-control module can be advantageous if you fulfil many sales orders every day.

Reviewer's Comment

There are a vast number of different fundraising initiatives that organisations are involved in. Database considerations should be discussed before beginning the initiative so that appropriate information can be captured and entered.

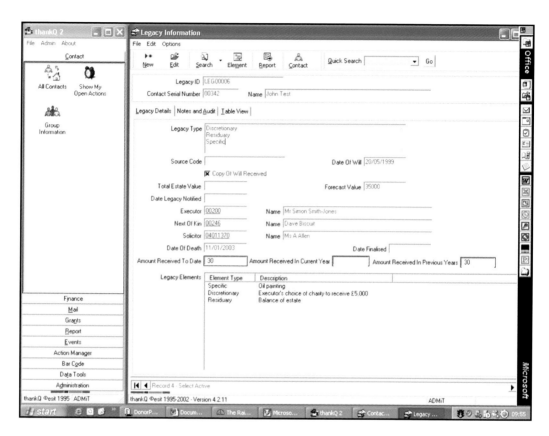

**Legacy administration data from
database thankQ**

HOW CAN THE DATABASE HELP?

Apart from who gave the money and when they gave it, two other concepts are very important with regard to evaluating sources of income. These concepts are what gave rise to the income (the campaign or appeal) and what the money is to be used for (the fund or project).

TECHNICAL CONSIDERATIONS

Campaigns and appeals

To manage the data related to a fundraising campaign or appeal, you need to record:

- ▪ A diary of actions to be carried out during the campaign.

- ▪ The name and type of the campaign.

- ▪ The number of people approached.

- ▪ The cost of the campaign.

- ▪ The projected income from the campaign.

- ▪ The running total of income received from the campaign.

The running total should be automatically updated by the system every time a donation is recorded against a supporter. By recording the number of approaches, the cost and the income received, you can report on the cost per approach, the cost per donation received and the overall return on investment.

Fundraising campaigns or appeals can often be constructed at a number of levels. A summer campaign may consist of a magazine insert, a telephone campaign and a mailing. Inserts can be placed in different publications, or the audiences for telephone or mailing approaches may be segmented into different groups that require separate analyses. It may be that different mailings or inserts are tested against one another. All these levels and combinations need to be recorded and evaluated.

Allocating funds

Money is often raised for specific purposes, and sometimes there is a legal obligation to use the money only for the purpose requested by the donor.

MANAGING CAMPAIGNS AND ALLOCATING FUNDS

Hence the construction of a table of funds/purposes/projects is necessary.

Managing funds is similar in many ways to managing campaigns. You need to record:

- The name and type of fund for which funds are being sought.

- The target income required.

- The income received.

- Specific requirements relating to the use of money raised for the fund.

Again, the income received should be updated automatically as each income item is entered. It is also useful to be able to record the amounts actually spent on the project to date, in order to know the balance of the fund. This is strictly an accounting function, but it is useful for fundraisers to know how a project is going and whether more money will be needed for a particular purpose.

As with campaigns, funds can also be separated at a number of levels. A three-level hierarchy is not uncommon (e.g., for an overseas aid agency: country, area and village).

Continues on next page

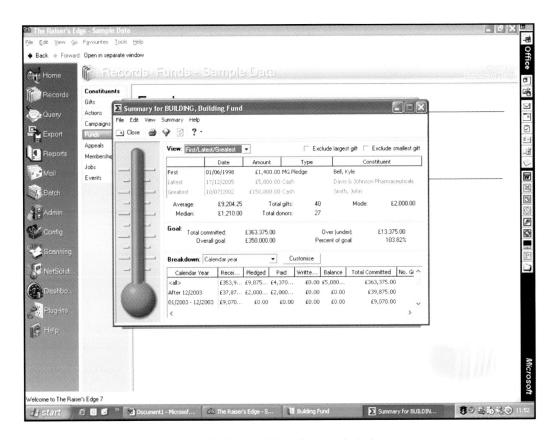

**Fund summary information from database
The Raiser's Edge**

FINAL THOUGHTS

By considering all the potential requirements of the database, and consulting widely with all the different user groups, it is possible for all teams to operate with one system, providing it is flexible. This facilitates cross-team communication, and adds real value to fundraising performance. Thus the database is a vital tool in monitoring and managing the communications going out from different departments, and in getting a full picture of what a supporter is doing for an NPO. It enables information to be stored in a controlled way, but with all those who need it having access. To achieve this it is important to plan for all the requirements that will be made of the database, and to give someone specific responsibility for managing it.

PETER FLORY, AUTHOR

Peter Flory is an independent Information Technology consultant. Peter spent nearly half his life in Australia and half in the UK. He has been in the computer industry since 1965. He has been a management consultant since 1981 and has specialised in charity and membership organisations since 1986. In 1989 he decided to become a completely independent business and IT consultant and formed Athena Consultants to provide the highest level of independent and ethical consultancy services to a wide range of clients. Since 1990 he has worked solely in the voluntary sector.

Peter spent eight years as a management consultant with BDO Binder Hamlyn after a sixteen-year career in the traditional IT areas of programming, systems analysis, project management and IT management. As a consultant he has handled many projects for all types of businesses from manufacturers, to retailers, to import/exporters, to insurance companies, to banks, to government departments. Assignments have ranged from feasibility studies and strategic direction analysis, through systems specification, evaluation, contract negotiation, project control and systems review. He is a "hands on" technical specialist too, numbering several programming languages in his repertoire and has experience in all the main operating systems and hardware platforms. He specialises in business improvement by determining how organisations can become more efficient through the effective use of technology.

Caroline Hukins, Reviewer

Caroline Hukins has worked in the non-profit sector in the UK for more than 10 years, both as a volunteer fundraiser and a professional.

Following university, she won a place on the National Society for the Prevention of Cruelty to Children (NSPCC) graduate trainee program in Fundraising Appeals, and subsequently worked on the multimillion-pound Full Stop Campaign for the Millennium. She spent 18 months organizing overseas biking and trekking challenges for Macmillan Cancer Relief, generating over $1 million from this type of fundraising. She then spent 3 years managing a wide-ranging events program at the National Asthma Campaign, which inclided sporting events, overseas challenges, sponsored activities, ticketed special events and wider community fundraising.

Caroline now works as a freelance author and editor, and leads charity treks and bike rides all over the world.